For centuries, tea has held a valued place in both Eastern and Western cultures. From the ritual of a Japanese tea ceremony to the cosy informality of an English cuppa at the kitchen table, tea — whether green, black, white or herbal — soothes, grounds and comforts us.

It's no surprise that so many of us switch on the kettle at the first sign of trouble — keep calm and drink tea! The mere act of pausing to sip a cup of tea is often enough to clear our mind and inspire some creative problem-solving. And then there are the medicinal benefits. Tea is rich in antioxidants, and numerous studies suggest that drinking tea may help to reduce our risk of heart attack and stroke, improve muscle endurance, protect our bones, boost our immune system, and even improve our skin and keep our smile bright!

More than any other beverage, it seems that tea unites people across nationalities, ages, races and gender. Six billion cups of tea are drunk every day around the world, and no matter whether you are rich or poor, an introvert or extrovert, a rock star or a dentist, chances are there's a blend of tea out there that's just right for you.

The quotes in this book certainly confirm that tea's appeal is universal. They include words of wisdom (and otherwise!) from people as diverse as Buddhist monks, politicians, actors and adventurers, with Thich Nhat Hanh, Mick Jagger, Abraham Lincoln, Audrey Hepburn, Billy Connolly and Bear Grylls being just a few of the notable names who have professed their love of tea.

It's hoped that the resulting book brings you the same pleasure as a perfectly brewed cup of your own particular favourite.

You can never get
a cup of tea large
enough or a book
long enough to
suit me.

C.S. LEWIS

Make tea, not war.

MONTY PYTHON

The perfect
temperature for tea
is two degrees hotter
than just right.

TERRI GUILLEMETS

Tea is quiet and our thirst
for tea is never far from our
craving for beauty.

JAMES NORWOOD PRATT

This morning's tea makes

yesterday distant.

TANKO

Tea is a divine herb.

XU GUANGQI

The most trying hours in life
are between four o'clock
and the evening meal. A cup
of tea at this time adds a lot
of comfort and happiness.

ROYAL S. COPELAND

Drinking a daily cup
of tea will surely starve
the apothecary.

CHINESE PROVERB

A cup of tea is a
cup of peace.

SOSHITSU SEN XV

Tea began as a
medicine and grew
into a beverage.

OKAKURA KAKUZO

Water is the mother of
tea, a teapot its father,
and fire the teacher.

CHINESE PROVERB

Bread and water can so
easily be toast and tea.

UNKNOWN

There is no need to have
any special attitude while
drinking except one of
thankfulness. The nature of
tea itself is that of no-mind.

POJONG SUNIM

Each cup of tea represents
an imaginary voyage.

CATHERINE DOUZEL

Tea is drunk to forget

the din of the world.

T'IEN YI-HENG

My hour for tea is half-past five, and my buttered toast waits for nobody.

WILKIE COLLINS

Drink your tea slowly and
reverently, as if it is the
axis on which the world
revolves — slowly, evenly,
without rushing toward
the future. Live the actual
moment. Only this
moment is life.

THICH NHAT HANH

There is no trouble
so great or grave
that cannot be much
diminished by
a nice cup of tea.

BERNARD-PAUL HEROUX

If you are cold, tea will warm you; if you are too heated, it will cool you; if you are depressed, it will cheer you; if you are excited, it will calm you.

WILLIAM EWART GLADSTONE

Teas vary as much
in appearance as the
different faces of men.

HUI-TSUNG

The Truth lies in

a bowl of tea.

NAMBO SOKEI

She had that brand of
pragmatism that would find
her the first brewing tea
after Armageddon.

CLIVE BARKER

Never trust a man who,

when left alone in a

room with a tea cozy,

doesn't try it on.

BILLY CONNOLLY

When I drink tea I am conscious of peace. The cool breath of heaven rises in my sleeves and blows my cares away.

LO TUNG

Tea cannot be learned
from a book, only from
the heart.

SOCHI

Great love affairs start
with Champagne and
end with tisane.

HONORÉ DE BALZAC

I take pleasure in tea,
appreciating it with my
spirit and therefore cannot
explain why.

SEN JOO

Strange how a teapot can
represent at the same time
the comforts of solitude and
the pleasures of company.

UNKNOWN

A crisis pauses during tea.

TERRI GUILLEMETS

Teaism is a cult founded on the adoration of the beautiful among the sordid facts of everyday existence ... It is essentially a worship of the Imperfect, as it is a tender attempt to accomplish something possible in this impossible thing we know as life.

OKAKURA KAKUZO

A Proper Tea is much nicer
than a Very Nearly Tea,
which is one you forget
about afterwards.

A.A. MILNE

Coffee is not my cup of tea.

SAMUEL GOLDWYN

A woman is like a tea
bag — you can't tell how
strong she is until you put
her in hot water.

ELEANOR ROOSEVELT

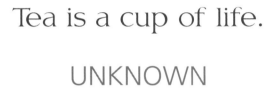

Tea is a cup of life.

UNKNOWN

If this is coffee, please
bring me some tea; but
if this is tea, please bring
me some coffee.

ABRAHAM LINCOLN

Tea is also a sort of spiritual
refreshment, an elixir
of clarity and wakeful
tranquility. No pleasure is
simpler, no luxury cheaper,
no consciousness-altering
agent more benign.

JAMES NORWOOD PRATT

A true warrior, like
tea, shows his strength
in hot water.

CHINESE PROVERB

Everything has a
beginning. I believe
I will begin with tea.

JENNIFER R. COOK

Iced tea is too pure and
natural a creation not to
have been invented as soon
as tea, ice, and hot
weather crossed paths.

JOHN EGERTON

If man has no tea
in him, he is incapable
of understanding truth
and beauty.

JAPANESE PROVERB

Come, let us have some
tea and continue to talk
about happy things.

CHAIM POTOK

Tea is instant wisdom,

just add water!

ASTRID ALAUDA

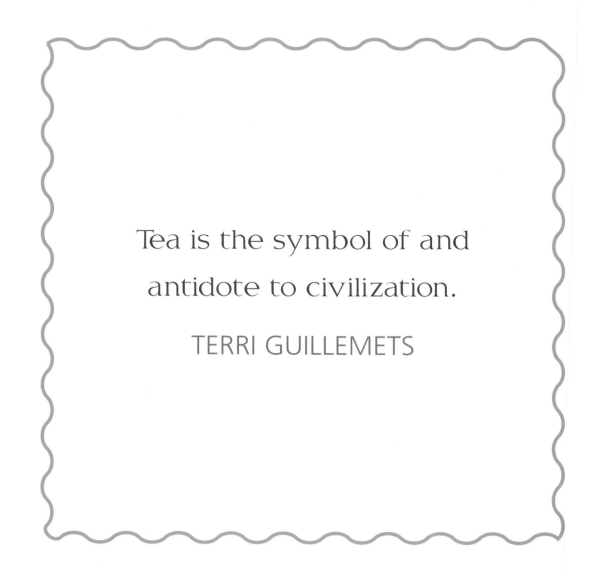

Tea is the symbol of and
antidote to civilization.

TERRI GUILLEMETS

I'm a green tea addict,
though the occasional glass
of red wine is nice, too.

SHILPA SHETTY

I got nasty habits;

I take tea at three.

MICK JAGGER

Tea is the elixir of life.

LAO TZU

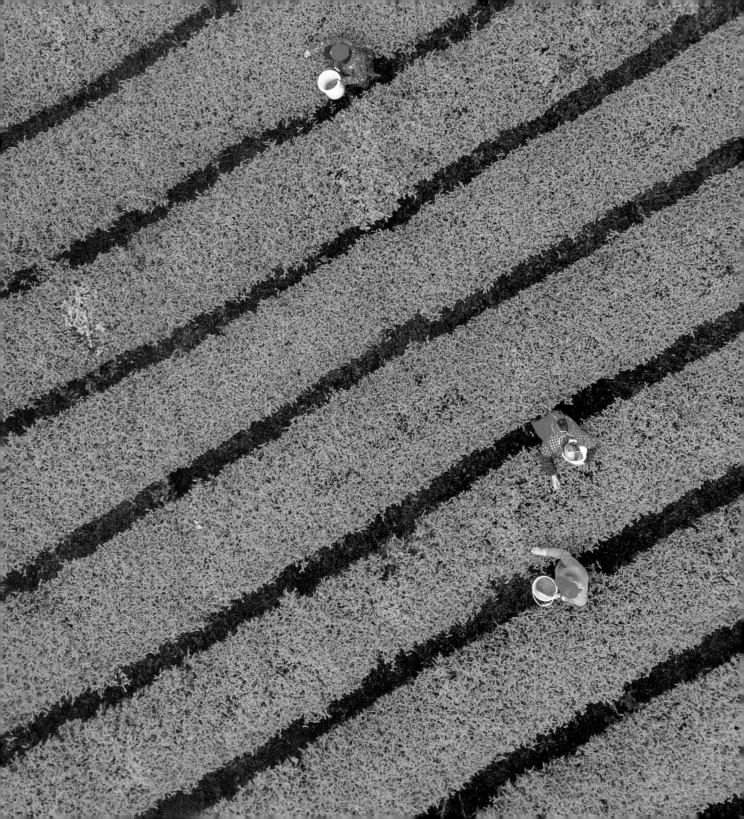

Tea is a beverage which not only quenches thirst, but dissipates sorrow.

CHANG LOO

There are those who love to get dirty and fix things. They drink coffee at dawn, beer after work. And those who stay clean, just appreciate things. At breakfast they have milk and juice at night. There are those who do both. They drink tea.

GARY SNYDER

When you have
nobody you can make
a cup of tea for,
when nobody needs
you, that's when
I think life is over.

AUDREY HEPBURN

There are few hours in
life more agreeable than
the hour dedicated to
the ceremony known as
afternoon tea.

HENRY JAMES

Brewing a good cuppa is something not everyone can do, and I loathe bad tea.

ROD STEWART

It has been well said
that tea is suggestive of
a thousand wants, from
which spring the decencies
and luxuries of civilization.

AGNES REPPLIER

I was always brought up to
have a cup of tea at halfway
up a rock face.

BEAR GRYLLS

There is nothing quite
like a freshly brewed pot
of tea to get you going
in the morning.

PHYLLIS LOGAN

I would rather have a cup
of tea than sex.

BOY GEORGE

Love and scandal are the best sweeteners of tea.

HENRY FIELDING

I like the pause that
tea allows.

WARIS AHLUWALIA

Tea makes everything
better.

BINDI IRWIN

I do hold very strongly that tea is better in England. There's something in the milk. They must have special cows.

GAIL CARRIGER

The grandfather plants and raises the tea bushes, the father harvests the tea, and the son drinks it.

CHINESE PROVERB

As the centerpiece of a
cherished ritual, it's
a talisman against the chill of
winter, a respite from the
ho-hum routine of the day.

SARAH ENGLER

A thoughtful cup of tea
brought to your bedside
each morning means
more to me than the huge
bouquet of flowers bought
once a year.

PENNY JORDAN

With a cup of tea in your hand, anything is possible.

UNKNOWN

Life is like a cup of tea; it's
all in how you make it.

UNKNOWN

Come and share a pot of
tea. My home is warm and
my friendship's free.

EMILIE BARNES

Remember the tea
kettle — it is always up
to its neck in hot water,
yet it still sings!

UNKNOWN

Tea is nought but this: first you heat the water, then you make the tea. Then you drink it properly. That is all you need to know.

SEN RIKYU

There is something in the
nature of tea that leads
us into a world of quiet
contemplation of life.

LIN YUTANG

All true tea lovers not only
like their tea strong, but like
it a little stronger with each
year that passes.

GEORGE ORWELL

Wouldn't it be
dreadful to live in a
country where they
didn't have tea?

NOEL COWARD

There is a great deal of
poetry and fine sentiment
in a chest of tea.

RALPH WALDO EMERSON

When you want tea,
tea it is. Coffee just
doesn't cut it.

J.W. FLOOD

When life gets tough, the
tough grab the kettle.

UNKNOWN

Ecstasy is a glass full
of tea and a piece of
sugar in the mouth.

ALEXANDER PUSHKIN

The path to heaven
passes through a teapot.

PROVERB

The music of tea is the
melody that soothes me.

MORGAN CHRISTIANSEN